HEBREWS

LECTIO DIVINA FOR YOUTH

HEBREWS

LECTIO DIVINA FOR YOUTH

ANCIENT FAITH SERIES

Barefoot Ministries®
Kansas City, Missouri

Copyright © 2008 by Barefoot Ministries®

ISBN 978-0-8341-5024-9

Written by Mark Haines
Editor: Mike Wonch
Assistant Editor: Robyn M. Boss
Cover Design: JR Caines
Interior Design: Sharon Page

Adapted from *Lectio Divina Bible Studies: Listening for God Through Hebrews*.

Mark Haines. *Lectio Divina Bible Studies: Listening for God Through Hebrews*. Indianapolis, IN: Wesleyan Publishing House and Beacon Hill Press of Kansas City, 2005.

Library of Congress Control Number: 2008929041

10 9 8 7 6 5 4 3 2 1

ABOUT THE
LECTIO DIVINA
BIBLE STUDIES

Lectio divina (pronounced lek-tsee-oh dih-vee-nuh) is a Latin phrase that means *sacred reading*. It is the ancient Christian practice of communicating with God through the reading and study of Scripture. Throughout history, great Christian leaders have used and adapted this ancient method of interpreting Scripture.

The idea behind *lectio divina* is to look at a Bible passage in such a way that Bible study becomes less about study and more about listening. The approach is designed to focus our attention on what God is saying to us through the Word. Through the process of *lectio divina* we not only read to understand with our minds, but we read to hear with our hearts and obey. It is a way of listening to God through His Word.

Some throughout history have said that *lectio divina* turns Bible study on its head—normally we read the Bible, but in *lectio divina, the Bible reads us*. That is probably a good way to describe it. It is God using His Word in a conversation with us to read into our lives and speak to our hearts.

In this series, we will use the traditional *lectio divina* model. We have expanded each component so that it can be used by both individuals and by groups. Each session in this study includes the following elements. (Latin words and their pronunciation are noted in parentheses.)

- **Reading** (*Lectio* "lek-tsee-oh"). We begin with a time of quieting ourselves prior to reading. Then we take a slow, careful reading of a passage of Scripture. We focus our minds on the central theme of the passage. When helpful, we read out loud or read the same passage over and over several times.

- **Meditation** (*Meditatio* "medi-tah-tsee-oh"). Next, we explore the meaning of the Bible passage. Here we dig deep to try to

understand all of what God might be saying to us. We think on
the passage. We explore the images, and pay attention to the
emotions and feelings that the passage provides. We put ourselves in the story. We look for particular words or phrases that
leap off the page as the Spirit begins to speak to us through the
Word.

- **Prayer** (*Oratio* "or-ah-tsee-oh"). As we meditate on the passage,
  we respond to God by communicating with Him. We specifical-
  ly ask God to speak to us through His Word. We begin to dialog
  with Him about what we have read. We express praise, thanks-
  giving, confession, or agreement to God. And we listen. We wait
  before Him in silence, allowing God the chance to speak.

- **Contemplation** (*Contemplatio* "con-tehm-plah-tsee-oh"). At this
  point in our conversation through the Word, we come to a
  place where we rest in the presence of God. Our study is now
  about receiving what He has said to us. Imagine two old friends
  who have just talked at length—and now without words, they
  just sit together and enjoy each other's presence. Having spent
  time listening to God, we know a little better how God is shap-
  ing the direction of our lives. Here there is a yielding of oneself
  to God's will. We resolve to act on the message of Scripture.

GROUP STUDY

This book is designed to be useful for both individual and group
study. To use this in a group, you may take one of several approaches:

- **Individual Study/Group Review**. Make sure each member of
  the group has a copy of the book. Have them read through one
  section during the week. (They will work through the same
  passage or portions of it each day that week.) Then, when you
  meet together, review what thoughts, notes, and insights the
  members of the group experienced in their individual study.
  Use the group questions at the end of the section as a guide.

- **Group Lectio**. Make sure each member of the group has a copy of the book. Have them read through one section during the week in individual study. When you meet together as a group, you will study the passage together through a reading form similar to lectio divina:

- First, **read the passage out loud several times to the group.** Group members respond by waiting in silence and letting God speak.
- **Second, have the passage read aloud again to the group once or twice more.** Use different group members for different voices, and have them read slowly. Group members listen for a word or two that speaks to them, and share it with the group. Break into smaller groups if appropriate.
- **Third, read the passage out loud again, and have the group pray together to ask God what He might be saying to each person, and to the group as a whole.** Go around and share what each person is learning from this process. At this point, review together the group questions at the end of the section.[1]

- **Lectio Divina Steps for Groups.** Make sure each member has a copy of the book. As a group, move through the study together, going through each of the parts: reading, mediation, prayer, and contemplation. Be sure to use the group questions at the end of the section.

The important thing about using *lectio divina* in a group is to remember that this is to be incarnational ("in the flesh")—in other words, we begin to live out the Word in our community. We carry God's Word in us, (in the flesh, or incarnate in us) and we carry that Word into our group to be lived out among them.

The *Lectio Divina Bible Studies* invite readers to slow down, read Scripture, meditate upon it, and prayerfully respond to God's Word.

---

1. Parts of the "Group Lectio" section adapted from Tony Jones, *The Sacred Way: Spiritual Practices for Everyday Life*, Grand Rapids: Zondervan, 2005, p. 54.

CONTENTS

INTRODUCTION

How often our circumstances appear large in our own eyes. It often blurs our vision, alters our perceptions, and takes our attention away from what is important. Sometimes our circumstances can turn us away from what we know to be true. These temptations were common when the writer of Hebrews wrote his words of caution and challenge.

The content of this book (probably written between A.D. 65 and 70) leads us to believe that the unnamed writer was addressing Jewish followers of Christ who were so tossed about by persecution from Jews and Romans that they were tempted to return to the familiarity of Old Testament law, consequently renouncing the name of Jesus.

The cure to this temptation can be found in Hebrews 12:2, "Let us fix our eyes on Jesus." Studying this Epistle will help us do just that. It is full of references to Old Testament passages that point to their fulfillment in the person and work of Jesus Christ. Its focus is on Jesus as God Incarnate, Son of Man, and Great High Priest who lives to intercede for us.

This letter shows how our Savior is working on our behalf today from His position at the right hand of God's throne. Its challenge to believers now, as then, is to focus on Jesus, stand firm in difficult days, and hold to the hope of a greater day in heaven. "For we do not have a high priest who is unable to sympathize with our weaknesses, but we have one who has been tempted in every way, just as we are—yet was without sin. Let us then approach the throne of grace with confidence, so that we may receive mercy and find grace to help us in our time of need" (4:15-16).

I WILL PAY ATTENTION

LISTENING FOR GOD THROUGH
HEBREWS 1:1—2:4

SUMMARY

God created us to live in intimate fellowship. Adam and Eve experienced that kind of relationship with Him and each other until they sinned. Genesis 3 records the events. Satan came in the form of a snake and lied to Adam and Eve. He implied that God had misled them by telling them that sin would kill them. They chose to believe the snake and ate the forbidden fruit. Their distrust and disobedience has been passed on to the entire human race.

God's solution was to begin revealing the truth about himself to our fallen race. His prophets were the first ones to proclaim God's message. Finally, Jesus came as both the message and the messenger. Anyone who wants to know what God is like can look to Jesus. By paying close attention to Jesus and His message, you will begin to experience the intimate fellowship with God you were intended to enjoy.

PREPARATION ⚜ FOCUS YOUR THOUGHTS

List three people that you go to for advice.

Why do you pay attention to these people?

What traits do these people have in common?

READING ⚜ HEAR THE WORD

The Book of Hebrews seems to have been written to Jewish believers in Jesus who were tempted to turn back to their old religious practices. The author is not identified, but he obviously knew a great deal about Judaism. To read Hebrews seems more like you're reading a sermon than a letter. Its theme is the superiority of Jesus. It challenges believers to follow Him faithfully. In this opening passage the author makes the statement that we must pay attention to Jesus.

In this study text you will see the following terms.

Prophets: These were men and women who proclaimed God's message to His people, particularly in Old Testament Israel.

Glory: This word refers to the brightness and the weight of God's obvious presence. The Lord's glory filled the Tabernacle when Moses dedicated it (Exod. 40:34).

Angels: These spiritual beings are God's messengers and servants who help His people. The author of Hebrews implies that they delivered the Law to Moses on Mount Sinai. So do Paul (in Gal. 3:19) and Stephen (in Acts 7:53).

Drift: This word is used to describe boats or ships without an anchor. They simply float away with the waves.

With these concepts in mind, read Hebrews 1:1—2:4 aloud. If you are participating in a group study, have one person read the text aloud.

MEDITATION ⚜ ENGAGE THE WORD

Meditate on Hebrews 1:1-4

The author contrasts the message of the prophets and the message of the Son. How was Jesus both the message and the messenger? What advantage does that give Him over the prophets? Why?

In what ways has God spoken to you? Which seems to be His favorite means of communicating with you? How do you know when God is speaking to you, and what He is saying? How do you respond?

List the traits and actions of the Son mentioned in these verses. How do these traits and actions compare to those of God? What do the findings show you about the relationship between Jesus and God?

Which of these traits or actions means the most to you today? Why are they significant to you?

Read the quote by Rick Warren. Do you think he means Jesus is God's last message? His best message? His ultimate message? Or His only self-revealing message? Explain how you came to that answer.

> God's glory is best seen in Jesus Christ. He, the Light of the world, illuminates God's nature. Because of Jesus, we are no longer in the dark about what God is really like.
>   —Rick Warren

The author of Hebrews tells us the Son is seated at God's right hand in heaven. What does that tell us about His position and authority? What does it say about His work of providing cleansing from our sin? How does your relationship with Jesus reflect His position in heaven? How has His work changed your life? What is Jesus' position in your own life?

Meditate on Hebrews 1:5-14

The author repeats the question "to which of the angels did God ever say . . . ?" in Hebrews 1:5 and 13. What is the suggested answer to these questions? Why do you think the author repeated the question in a different way? How does this question support his argument about the Son being superior to the angels?

What does God say about the angels in Hebrews 1:7? How is that different from what He says about the Son in Hebrews 1:8-12? What do these statements tell us about Jesus?

Read what John Wesley wrote about angels. How does this statement compare to Hebrews 1:14? What is suggested about the relationship between angels and Christians?

John Wesley wrote that angels minister before God and are "sent forth to attend to men."
—Explanatory Notes on the New Testament

Why do you think angels and prophets might have been distracting to these Jewish Christians? Why would people be tempted to follow angels instead of Jesus?

What kinds of religious ideas can distract you from faithfully following Jesus? Why? How can you resist that temptation?

Meditate on Hebrews 2:1-4

The author tells us "we must pay more careful attention" to the message Jesus brought. What is the danger of not paying attention?

What happened to those who ignored the angels' message? What is the implied answer to the question in Hebrews 2:3? How do you feel about the author using that kind of motivation in a call to pay close attention to Jesus? Why?

The author indicates that Jesus delivered the message that demands close attention. Since only a few people met Him face-to-face, how can His message be confirmed to us? How has God testified to the authenticity of Jesus' message in your life?

Read Matthew Henry's quote. In a world that believes all religions lead to God, what provides the foundation for your faith in Jesus? What keeps you from drifting away in the current of this so-called tolerance?

> It was the will of God that we should have a sure footing for our faith, and a strong foundation for our hope in receiving the gospel.   —Matthew Henry

Read the observation about spiritual uncertainty on page 19. In what ways has God used insecurity and doubt to draw you into a deeper relationship with Jesus? What, if any, questions are you struggling with today?

> *Spiritual uncertainty is like the silent red light on the instrument panel of an automobile. It flashes its warning to tell us the oil is low and there is imminent danger to the motor. Under these conditions the very lack of assurance for which our hearts hunger is one more of God's gifts of grace to us.* —A. F. Harper

PRAYER ⚜ ASK AND LISTEN

Seek the face of God. Ask, "Lord, what are You saying to us today?"

Thank God for sending Jesus to purify you from sin. Listen for the Spirit's assurance of your salvation.

CONTEMPLATION ⚜ REFLECT AND YIELD

In what areas of your life do you need to pay more careful attention? Why?

How does the warning in this passage affect your desire to stand firm in your faith?

GROUP STUDY

- What are your thoughts on angels? As a group, discuss what comes to your mind when you think of angels.

- In what ways is Jesus superior to the angels?

- Knowing that the angels worship Jesus, what should our response be to Him?

- What does this chapter say about Jesus?

- When and how did the message of Jesus bring salvation to you?

- Find a quiet place. Pray, "Speak Lord, for Your servant is listening."

HE KNOWS MY PAIN

LISTENING FOR GOD THROUGH
HEBREWS 2:5-18

SUMMARY

This text will remind you of the honor God created us to experience. You will also see the lengths taken by Jesus so that we may be restored. The Son of God did not avoid any of the pain that was inevitable when living life in a fallen world. He took it all in.

The same Son introduced in Hebrews 1:1-4 as "the exact representation of God" became just like us. He experienced every part of life and death as a flesh-and-blood human being.

It's been said that the Son of God became human so human beings could become the children of God. These verses show us the truth in that statement. Hebrews 2:5-18 will urge you to believe that Jesus knows all about your sorrows. He was tempted so He can help you. Jesus suffered and died so He can identify with you in every way.

PREPARATION ✟ FOCUS YOUR THOUGHTS

Read Charles Wesley's comments on the Crucifixion.

> My Lord, my Love, is crucified! / Is Crucified for me and
> you, / To bring us rebels back to God; / Believe, believe
> the record true, / Ye all are bought with Jesus' blood; /
> Pardon for all flows from His side; / My Lord, my Love,
> is crucified!   —Charles Wesley

When you think about the Cross and God dying there for
you, what are your thoughts and feelings? What does it moti-
vate you to do?

READING ✟ HEAR THE WORD

This passage is an explanation of David's captivated response
to God's creation, found in Psalm 8. God intended for humans to rule over His physical creation. He planned for our
race to manage this world and to answer only to Him. Adam
and Eve surrendered that place of honor to Satan when they
sinned.

As these verses continue to develop the author's argument
that Jesus is superior to the angels, they show how He con-
quered Satan and re-established fallen humanity by becoming

one of us. He fulfilled humanity's role in ruling creation so the angels do not have dominion in God's kingdom. He can identify with us in such a way that we have become His brothers and sisters.

You will find these terms in Hebrews 2:5-18.

World to come: These words refer to Christ's future reign in "a new heaven and a new earth" where "there will be no more death or mourning or crying or pain" (Rev. 21:1-14).

Grace: This refers to God giving to us something we do not deserve, cannot earn, and can never repay.

Make holy: This is sanctification. It is Christ's work in our lives that changes our inner being and then our behavior. It is everything God does to make us more like Jesus.

Atonement: This is the effect of a sacrifice in taking away both God's judgment and the sin that causes it.

MEDITATION ⸙ ENGAGE THE WORD

Meditate on Hebrews 2:5-9

Hebrews 2:6-8 quotes from Psalm 8. The *Revised Standard Version* translates Psalm 8:5 as, "Yet thou hast made him a little less than God." How does this view compare to your view of humankind?

Read the commentary on Psalm 8:5. Do you see yourself as "puny and insignificant" or as a person bearing God's image with glory and royal authority? Why do you think as you do?

> Far from puny and insignificant, we have been made in God's image, crowned with His glory, and set over our own kingdom. Some object to this description. They warn against putting too much emphasis on human ability and observe that whatever glory humanity had at the beginning was lost in the Fall. While sin has considerably hampered progress, the description in Psalm 8 describes . . . the son of man . . . a term that refers to humankind outside the Garden of Eden.
>
> —Stephen J. Lennox

The author of Hebrews writes that God has ranked humans right below Him. If God put everything under humankind, why is it that "we do not see everything subject" to us? Who is in control of this world now? Why?

Jesus stands in contrast to the rest of humanity. In what ways was Jesus made a little lower than the angels? What did He receive as a result of suffering and dying? What does the author imply when he writes that Jesus tasted death for everyone?

Read Philippians 2:5-11. How do those verses compare to the thoughts of Hebrews 2:5-9? In Philippians 2:5 we are commanded to have the same attitude as Jesus. How would you describe that attitude? How did Jesus view himself? What was His motivation for becoming a human being? Why did He choose to die on the Cross? If you had the same attitude toward God, toward yourself, and toward others as Jesus had, what would it mean in your life? What, if anything, would you need to change? How would you relate to God and others differently?

Meditate on Hebrews 2:10-13

The word *glory* appears three times in Hebrews 2:5-10. The author of Hebrews said Jesus is "the radiance of God's glory" in Hebrews 1:3. Use a Bible dictionary to discover the meaning of this word. If you are participating in a group, read the definition aloud and discuss your thoughts. What does the meaning of *glory* tell you about God's goal for you?

Read Hebrews 5:8, and compare it to Hebrews 2:10. What do they have in common?

Read John Piper's quote on page 26. How can you explain the fact that God made Jesus the author of our salvation through suffering? Do you think it is right for us to benefit from Jesus' pain? What other meanings could this verse have? Would any of these alternatives make sense in this context? Why, or why not?

> When the Bible says that Jesus "learned obedience through what he suffered," it . . . means that with each new trial he learned in practice—and in pain—what it means to obey. When it says that he was "made perfect through suffering," it . . . means that he was gradually fulfilling the perfect righteousness that he had to have in order to save us.   —John Piper

What does it mean to be holy? In what ways is God holy? In what ways was Jesus holy? In what ways are you holy? If you are doing a group study, talk with the other members about a time when you experienced Jesus' power to make you holy in some area of your life.

Paul often referred to himself a slave of Jesus Christ. Hebrews 2:11 declares that we are brothers and sisters with Jesus in God's family. What is the difference between a slave and a child? How do you feel about Jesus calling you brother or sister? What does being a sibling of Jesus imply about your relationships with other Christians?

Meditate on Hebrews 2:14-18

Jesus shared our humanity. God the Son became a flesh-and-blood man. Theologians call this unique event the Incarnation. Compare these verses with Colossians 2:13-15. How did

Jesus destroy the devil? How did He set us free from the fear of death?

Read about the Incarnation. What would happen in your life if you were completely convinced that God would be a "committed participant" with you?

> Incarnation is God's promise to be a committed participant with us in our living, our imagining, our dreaming, and our yearning.   —W. Paul Jones

Do you really believe Jesus suffered when He was tempted? Do you think Jesus could help you in your temptations if He had not suffered through it himself? Why, or why not?

PRAYER ♱ ASK AND LISTEN

Seek the face of God. Ask, "Lord, what are You saying to us today?"

Pray a sentence prayer aloud that welcomes God to join your everyday living, dreaming, and planning. Listen for His promise to be a committed participant with you.

CONTEMPLATION ✠ REFLECT AND YIELD

In which of your dreams and plans do you think God feels most free to participate? On which ones have you been flying solo? Surrender all of your dreams and plans to Jesus.

GROUP STUDY

- Why is it important to know that Jesus suffered and was tempted so He could relate to our struggles?

- Think about a time when Jesus helped you during a personal trial. How did it help strengthen your faith?

- How does it make you feel to realize that we benefited from Jesus' suffering?

- How does knowing that Jesus suffered for us make you want to live your life?

- How does it make you feel to think of Jesus as your brother?

- How would your life change if you expected Jesus to be a committed partner in all your decisions?

I WILL OBEY
LISTENING FOR GOD THROUGH
HEBREWS 3:1-19

SUMMARY

All the world's religions begin with the concept of separation. It could be separation from God, or from a peaceful spiritual mind-set, but we all want to know how to cross the bridge of where we are to where we want to be. The answer to that question is pretty consistent in all religions except for Christianity. Most religions teach that obedience to a set of rules will take you to the next level of where you want to be. Disobedience only carries you further away from that goal.

In contrast to other religions, the message of Hebrews 3 tells us that God bridged the gap through Jesus. Our response is simply to trust in Him. Trust establishes our relationship with God. Then we obey out of love and faithfulness to our Father God. So, the key for Christians is a question of trust. Obedience will flow from the answer to that question.

PREPARATION ✠ FOCUS YOUR THOUGHTS

You haven't been out of your childhood years for long, but think back to that time. Would your parents describe you as a strong-willed child? Do you feel like they would describe you as a strong-willed teen? If you are participating in a group, tell about a time when you refused to do what you were told.

READING ✠ HEAR THE WORD

Hebrews was written to encourage Jewish believers to stay faithful to Jesus in the midst of trials and persecution. The author begins Hebrews by describing Jesus in terms that allow the reader to become aware of His divinity. Then he calls us to pay careful attention to Jesus' message in order to avoid drifting away.

In Hebrews 3 the author calls his readers to focus on Jesus. He warns them of the danger of unbelief and unfaithfulness. Hebrews 3 cites the rebellion of the Israelites when they refused to enter the Promised Land (Num. 14). Those people did not believe God could or would help them possess the land, so they refused to go in.

The author states twice that what Jesus has done for us is conditional. If we hold on to our hope, and if we hold firmly until the end, we will share in His glory. We need to encourage each other to remain strong in our faith.

The following terms are keys to understanding this passage.

Faithful: A faithful person trusts God and is filled with faith in Him. The concept also implies that the faithful person acts in a trustworthy, dependable manner.

Hope: This is our confident expectation of all God has promised in Jesus.

Unbelief: This is the opposite of faith. An unbelieving person does not trust God and so refuses to obey Him.

MEDITATION ✿ Engage the Word

Meditate on Hebrews 3:1-6

Jesus is God's Son. He became a human to suffer and die for everyone. He has destroyed the devil and set us free from the fear of death. He has brought us into God's family, so we must set our sights on Him. Why would the author call for this request of Hebrews 1 and 2? How would this help his readers?

Jesus is called *Apostle* and *High Priest*. What kind of ministry does each of these titles imply? How do they encourage you to focus on Jesus?

Make a mental list to compare Jesus to Moses. How are they like each other? How are they different? Why was this comparison made? How would it encourage faithfulness?

Jesus built God's house. What are the requirements for being included in God's house?

In what situations have you been tempted to let go of your hope in Jesus? How have you managed to maintain a firm grasp of your courage in those times?

Meditate on Hebrews 3:7-15

Since there is a condition for receiving God's promises, we can't let ourselves make the same mistakes of those who rebelled against God. They heard His command to enter the Promised Land but refused to go in. What happened to Israel when they rebelled? In your opinion what is implied by the phrase "harden your hearts"? How would you describe your heart today? Why?

Read Numbers 14 and Psalm 95. How do these Old Testament passages reflect the need to hold firm to our faith? How can you explain the fact that the ones who refused to enter the Promised Land had seen the plagues in Egypt, walked through the Red Sea on dry ground, and heard God's thundering voice at Mount Sinai, but despite all those things, couldn't follow through with His request?

Read the quote about sin on page 33. Do you agree with this definition? Why? How does it compare to what the author of Hebrews says about unbelief and sin?

> *Sin is . . . the unwillingness of man to acknowledge his*
> *. . . dependence upon God and his effort to make his*
> *own life independent and secure.* —Reinhold Niebuhr

Hebrews 3:12-13 indicates that the cure for unbelief, sin, and hard hearts is found in an encouraging fellowship. Have you ever turned away from the living God to build your own independent life? What were the results? Did a fellow believer help you back? If so, how? What recommendations would you make to someone wanting to encourage a wandering brother or sister?

Read the statement by Rick Warren. What part should God's family play in encouraging your faithfulness? Can you share an example of a time when you either gave or received encouragement?

> *"Mind your own business" is not a Christian phrase.*
> *We are called and commanded to be involved in each*
> *other's lives.* —Rick Warren

There is a condition for sharing in Christ and His blessings. What must you do to participate in the blessings Jesus came to give?

Meditate on Hebrews 3:16-19

Read the quote about obedience by Henry Blackaby and Claude King. In what ways was Israel's rebellion a moment of truth for the nation? What was the result of their disobedience? What did their disobedience reveal about their view of God? Have you ever thought of your decisions in this way? How will this concept of belief producing obedience shape your future choices?

> In many ways, obedience is your moment of truth. What you do will: (1) Reveal what you believe about Him. (2) Determine whether you will experience His might in and through you. (3) Determine whether you come to know Him more intimately.
>
> —Henry Blackaby and Claude King

PRAYER ⚜ ASK AND LISTEN

Seek the face of God. Ask, "Lord, what are You saying to us today?"

Find a prayer partner to discuss any areas where you struggle to trust God enough to obey Him. Intercede for each other. Listen for Jesus' voice of gentle encouragement.

CONTEMPLATION ☩ Reflect and Yield

Think back over the last two weeks. When was your most recent moment of truth? Did you trust and obey? If you did, thank God for His help. Did you disobey? If you did, confess your sin and receive His cleansing forgiveness.

Group Study

- Do you think that obeying the rules and doing good deeds is all it takes to get closer to God and gain spiritual maturity, or is there more to it than that?

- What more does it take to reach a new level in terms of your spiritual growth? How do you grow in your personal faith?

- What makes you want to obey? Is it just because you want to be rewarded in the end, or does it come from a deeper love for Jesus?

- Discuss a time in your life when you didn't obey God. How did it make you feel to know you disregarded His command?

- How have you taken a leap of faith and obeyed God? Was it a hard thing to do? Why, or why not?

- Think of one way this week, as you go through your daily routine, you can allow more of God's presence to guide your life.

1 ENJOY GOD'S PRESENCE
LISTENING FOR GOD THROUGH
HEBREWS 4:1-16

SUMMARY

Israel had been refused entrance into the Promised Land because of unbelief. Hebrews 3:18-19 points out that the people failed to enter God's *rest*. Beginning there and continuing through most of chapter 4, the author uses the word *rest* in three different ways. The first way symbolizes the Promised Land along with its release from oppression and freedom to worship the Lord. The second use signifies the Sabbath Day established by God at the end of Creation. Both of these uses are illustrations of the third use, which shows the freedom from sin that only Jesus can supply. It gives us the right to enjoy His presence as we live and worship. The fullest experience of this rest will be found in heaven. However, you will discover that you can still enjoy God's rest in the here and now.

PREPARATION ✝ FOCUS YOUR THOUGHTS

When do you feel closest to God? How is this time different from other times?

Where do you go to find peace? What makes that place special?

Finish this sentence: "I feel most comfortable with God . . ."

READING ✝ HEAR THE WORD

The following words and phrases are important in Hebrews 4.

Gospel: The good news of God's promised blessings. In this passage it applies to both Old Testament and New Testament promises.

Joshua: The successor to Moses who led Israel into the Promised Land 40 years after the rebellion. *Jesus* is the Greek form of *Joshua.* So the author contrasts Joshua the Old Testament hero with Joshua the Son of God.

Throne of grace: The center of God's power and authority where He gives His blessings to undeserving people.

Mercy: This is forgiveness for all sins.

MEDITATION ✠ ENGAGE THE WORD

Meditate on Hebrews 4:1-5

Israel refused to enter God's rest, but God's offer is still open. So the author calls readers to make sure they, too, do not fall short of His rest. What similarities are there between the gospel we have heard and the gospel Israel heard before its rebellion? Why did the message they heard fail to be of value to them? What will happen if you have faith in the gospel you've heard?

Read Genesis 2:1-3. What is the relationship between the rest refused by Israel, the rest of God on the seventh day, and the rest that remains for the believer?

Meditate on Hebrews 4:6-11

The people of Israel heard God's message but did not combine it with faith. They disobeyed His command, and they missed out on His rest.

How is this open promise of rest encouraging to you? What benefits do you expect to experience if you enter God's rest? What kind of work will you rest from? Is it the work of trying to earn His acceptance and approval? If so, why can you rest from it?

Read the statement by A. F. Harper on page 40. What does he

consider the key to entering God's rest? Have you committed your all to God and His loving care? If not, what seems to keep you from doing so? In what ways are you struggling to trust God to care for you?

> Having committed my all to God, I rest. He cares for me. No final harm can come to me while I lean back on Him. —A. F. Harper

The *Amplified New Testament* puts Hebrews 4:11 like this: "Let us therefore be zealous *and* exert ourselves *and* strive diligently to enter in that rest [of God]—to know and experience it for ourselves." What level of priority do the words *zealous, exert,* and *strive diligently* seem to convey? Is knowing and experiencing God's rest a high priority to you? Or is it just an interesting topic for discussion in a Bible study? What would happen if you made entering God's rest your top priority?

The goal of entering God's rest is to keep everyone from disobedience. Do you think of the Christian life as something you go through alone or is it a team effort? What are the pros and cons of each point of view?

Meditate on Hebrews 4:12-16

To truly experience God's rest takes effort because we cannot fake our way into it. God's Word will not allow it. In what ways is the Word of God "living and active"? Tell about a time when you had to evaluate your thoughts and attitudes based on God's Word.

In Psalm 139:7-18 the psalmist takes comfort from God's uninterrupted presence in his life. Are you reassured by the idea that no part of your life is hidden from God? How does knowing He sees everything about you affect your decisions and behavior? Why?

List the unique qualifications of Jesus that make Him our Great High Priest. Which one makes Him seem most accessible to you? Why?

Read the quote about Jesus' temptations. Is it difficult to stand firm against temptation? What makes giving into temptation easier than resisting it? What temptations do you find are an endless battle? What would you expect from someone who was victorious over the temptations you struggle with often? What does Jesus promise?

> On the way to the cross for thirty years, Christ was tempted like every human is tempted. True, he never sinned. But wise people have pointed out that this means His temptations were stronger than ours, not weaker. —John Piper

Read the statement by A. W. Tozer. Do you believe God's mercy is available for every weakness, mistake, and sin in your life? Do you feel like you are able to enter His presence boldly and joyfully? Explain your answer.

> *To receive mercy we must first know that God is merciful. And it is not enough to believe that He once showed mercy to Noah or Abraham or David and will again show mercy in some future happy day. We must believe that God's mercy is boundless, free and, through Jesus Christ our Lord, available to us now in our present situation.* —A. W. Tozer

PRAYER ☦ ASK AND LISTEN

Seek the face of God. Ask, "Lord, what are You saying to us today?"

Meditate on this song lyric: *Just as I am, You will welcome and receive.* Listen for God's loving voice as He welcomes you home.

CONTEMPLATION ☦ REFLECT AND YIELD

Is there an attitude or habit that you feel uncomfortable about in Jesus' presence? Are you willing to admit that to Him? Will you surrender it and receive His mercy and grace?

Group Study

- What does it mean to you to find "rest" in God?

- What are some things that you struggle with in this world that you would like to find rest from?

- How would your youth group dynamic change if you all made finding rest in God your top priority?

- What are some ways that you can work on making this your top priority?

- Discuss areas in your life you want to give fully to God.

- What part of this chapter has had the most impact on your heart?

- How has this chapter encouraged you to change your attitudes and actions?

- Break into smaller groups of two. Pray for one another, and commit to be an accountability partner, helping your partner through the rough areas of his or her life.

I AM COMPLETELY SAVED
LISTENING FOR GOD THROUGH
HEBREWS 7:11-28

SUMMARY

The holiest place in the Temple was the inner room. It was thought of as God's throne room on earth. Gentiles could not enter the Temple. Jewish women were only allowed in the courtyard. Jewish men could go into an area a little closer to the holiest place. The priests were the only ones allowed in the area surrounding the holiest place. But access to that inner room was granted only to the high priest on one day each year.

Jesus is our Great High Priest. He surpasses the priesthood of the Old Testament system, because He accomplished what it could not. Jesus took away all the guilt and penalty of sin. He removed that barrier between God and us. He ushers everyone who believes in Him into heaven's throne room.

You will not be excluded when you come to Him by faith. As you study, you will find a comfort deep inside. Jesus saves you completely.

PREPARATION ✞ FOCUS YOUR THOUGHTS

If you could change one thing about your past, what would it be? How would that change affect you now? Explain your reasons for wanting this change.

READING ✞ HEAR THE WORD

The author of Hebrews has said that you were created to enjoy God's presence, but sin stops that from happening. So Jesus became the Great High Priest. By experiencing all of life's temptations and pain, ending in His death on a cross, Jesus opened the promise of resting in God's presence to everyone.

This would have raised questions in the mind of his Jewish audience. God established the Levitical priesthood. Each priest had to prove he was a direct descendant of Aaron, the first high priest. The sacrificial system at the Temple had been in effect for more than a thousand years. Jesus was not a descendant of Aaron. How could Jesus be the Great High Priest? Why would God change the very system He had started?

The author answers these questions in Hebrews 7:11-28.

You will see these terms in this text.

Perfect: We tend to think of *perfect* as meaning *flawless, fault-less,* or *unspoiled.* However, in the Bible *perfect* and its various forms refer to a person or thing that accomplishes the purpose for which it was intended. For example, a hammer is perfect for driving nails; but even a flawless hammer is not perfect for stirring cake batter.

Melchizedek: A non-Jewish priest of God to whom Abraham paid a tithe (Gen. 14:18-20 and Heb. 7:1-10).

MEDITATION ✝ ENGAGE THE WORD

Meditate on Hebrews 7:11-17

The Levitical priesthood could not see "perfect fellowship between God and the worshipper" (AMP.). Therefore, a new priest and a new order were needed. We need a priest who can lead us into God's presence with confidence and joy.

Read Hebrews 7:1-10. How are Melchizedek and Jesus similar? How are they different? In what ways are they superior to the Levitical priesthood?

How would you describe perfect fellowship with God to a young child? How would you describe it to the others in your youth group? How do you explain it to yourself?

Read the quote from William Barclay on page 48. If the goal of religion is free access to God, what barriers did the Levitical priesthood fail to remove? What limited the effectiveness of those priests? Would you have been satisfied with the end result of their ritual?

> As we read this passage we have to remember the basic idea of religion which never leaves the mind of the writer to the Hebrews. To him religion is access to God's presence as friends, with nothing between us and Him.　　　　　　　　　　　—William Barclay

Find and examine a diagram of the Temple in Jerusalem. Who had access to God's presence? How close to the holiest place would you have been able to go?

Why do you suppose the holiest place was off-limits to almost everyone? Read Matthew 27:50-51. What does that say about the whole system of laws and rituals surrounding the Temple?

Meditate on Hebrews 7:18-22

Think about the lives of Melchizedek, Aaron, and Jesus. What similarities do you see? What differences? Why are the differences significant? If you are participating in a group, break into smaller groups and make these charts, and then share what you have discovered.

In what ways did the Law fail? Have you tried to gain access to God's presence through your own good deeds and religious acts? What caused you to realize that it wouldn't work? Have you found peace in God's presence through Jesus? If you are in a group, share your stories with one another.

Meditate on Hebrews 7:23-28

What prevented other priests from continuing in office? Why isn't Jesus limited in the same way? What is the result of Jesus' ministry as our priest? Are you comforted and encouraged by the strength of Jesus' priesthood? Why?

Read the statement by A. F. Harper. What are some reasons he might believe that? What difference does it make in terms of your security with God that Jesus "is able to save completely"? How does it affect your daily decisions and activities? What does it do to your desire to follow Jesus? Why?

> Christ has the power to save us completely and perfectly. He can save us not only from the guilt and punishment of sin, but also from its nature and power.
>
> —A. F. Harper

Read George Buttrick's statement about intercession on page 50. Do you believe Jesus' intercession for you is specific?

Does Jesus bear your burden in His heart? How would it make you feel if you could hear His prayers for you? Explain.

Intercession is more than just specific, it is pondered; it requires us to bear on our heart the burden of those for whom we pray. —George Buttrick

According to Hebrews 7:26-28, what can Jesus do that no other priest can do? What character qualities set Him apart from Levitical priests? How is His sacrifice superior to theirs? Why was Jesus' sacrifice a "once for all" event? How does that benefit you?

Summarize the author's argument for the superiority of Jesus' priesthood. Make this your own personal statement. Begin by finishing this sentence. "Jesus is the only priest who can meet my needs, because . . ."

PRAYER ✙ ASK AND LISTEN

Seek the face of God. Ask, "Lord, what are You saying to us today?"

Get with a partner and pray for the areas in your life that are hard to give completely to God. Be accountable to each other, and ask the Lord to help you release these things as you go throughout your week.

CONTEMPLATION ☦ REFLECT AND YIELD

What old ways tempt you to turn away from Jesus? How is He better than those old ways?

GROUP STUDY

- How is our definition of "perfect" different from the way "perfect" is used in Hebrews?

- Discuss how your life would change if you thought of the word "perfect" as how it is described in the Bible.

- Would thinking of "perfect" in that way cause you to be more at peace with yourself?

- Is there any area of your life where you struggle to earn God's acceptance and approval?

- Why have you found it hard to entrust this into the hands of Jesus?

- What spoke to you the most during this chapter of the Bible study? Why was this so meaningful to you?

- With your group, discuss what it means to have our sins completely forgiven by God. How will knowing you are completely forgiven affect the way you live this week?

I AM HIS AND HE IS MINE
LISTENING FOR GOD THROUGH
HEBREWS 8:1-13; 9:11-15

SUMMARY

Jesus established a new covenant between God and humans
by dying on the Cross. This agreement with God promises to
clear our hearts of guilt and shame. The Old Testament sacrifices provided atonement, or covering, for sin. This made individuals ritually clean so they could fellowship with God.
However, these rituals couldn't erase the sin and the guilt and
the shame it caused. Their consciences were not clean.

The new covenant, brought by Jesus, allows us to have an intimate relationship with God. The covenant with Israel was
based on obedience to the Law. The rebellious attitude in all
humans prevented the Israelites from keeping the covenant,
so they could not experience intimacy with God.

As you study the new covenant you will discover that Jesus can change that rebellious attitude and write the law of love on your heart. You will experience the thrill of knowing that you are His and He is yours.

PREPARATION ✝ FOCUS YOUR THOUGHTS

After a wedding, can a couple honestly say they belong to each other? Why?

How does the relationship of a married couple change over time?

In what ways might your relationship with God change over time?

READING ✝ HEAR THE WORD

Human beings were created for an intimate relationship with God. However, sin separated us from Him. Even so, the Lord promised the Israelites that He would walk among them; He would be their God, and they would be His people if they obeyed His commands. For hundreds of years, Israel thought that the Temple fulfilled that promise. However, the destruction of Jerusalem in 587 B.C. brought that to an end.

The prophets Jeremiah, Ezekiel, Joel, and Zechariah stirred up Israel's hunger for this intimate relationship once again.

Over and over, God promised to change His people from the inside out. For example, Ezekiel 11:19-20 says, "I will give them an individual heart and put a new spirit in them; I will remove from them their heart of stone and give them a heart of flesh. Then they will follow my decrees and be careful to keep my laws. They will be my people, and I will be their God." The prophet Jeremiah says something similar in the passage quoted by the writer to the Hebrews in this text.

The following are key terms to understand in this passage.

Covenant: This is an agreement voluntarily entered by two parties. God sets the conditions for gaining access to His presence. Everyone who meets those conditions will be His people, and He will be their God.

Mediator: A person who negotiates and institutes agreements between two parties.

MEDITATION ☦ Engage the Word

Meditate on Hebrews 8:1-7

Review Hebrews 7:26. What makes Jesus the High Priest we need? In this section of Hebrews 8, what two descriptions does the author add in regard to Jesus?

Is Jesus the only person who can function as the High Priest we need? Has any other religious leader met the same qualifications? How would you communicate this truth to someone of a different religion?

How are the places, structures, and assignments of the two priesthoods contrasted in these verses? Why did Moses need to follow God's pattern for the Tabernacle precisely?

Think about your own patterns of worship. In what ways do they reflect worship in heaven's sanctuary?

Meditate on Hebrews 8:7-13

If the goal of the first covenant was to restore the relationship between God and humans, why was a new covenant needed? What was wrong with the first one? In your opinion, why didn't God start with the second covenant?

What was God's reason for establishing a different covenant? List the blessings you can receive in the new covenant. Rank them in the order of what seems most helpful to you at this time. If you are participating in a group study, discuss the list that you have come up with.

Read the commitment prayer from John Wesley's *Covenant Service* on page 57. What are the suggestions for each of the promises Wesley called the early Methodists to make?

I am no longer my own, but Yours. Put me to what You
will, rank me with whom You will; put me to doing, put
me to suffering; let me be employed for You or laid
aside for You, praised for You or humbled for You; let me
be full, let me be empty; let me have all things, let me
have nothing; I freely and cheerfully yield all things to
Your pleasure and disposal. —John Wesley

What possible changes might you see God make in your life
if you pray these promises? How do you feel about the idea
of giving God full authority in your life? Why?

Read Matthew Henry's statement, and compare it to Jesus'
words in Luke 22:19-20. Have you been baptized? What
kinds of promises and commitments are made in a baptismal
service? Do you find Communion to be a time of renewal
and commitment? Why?

The articles of this covenant . . . are sealed between
God and His people by baptism and the Lord's Supper;
whereby they bind themselves to their part, and God
assures them He will do His part; and His is the main
and principle part, on which His people depend for
grace and strength to do them. —Matthew Henry

Meditate on Hebrews 9:11-15

Where does Jesus carry out His priestly duties? How did He gain entrance to the Tabernacle? Does the phrase "once for all" refer to all persons? all sins? all time? all believers? something else?

What did the blood and ashes of animals do for the Israelites? What can Jesus' blood do for us?

Read the quote by John Piper. Have you ever experienced a guilty conscience and found relief in Jesus' blood? If you are in a group study, share your personal stories.

> When our conscience rises up and condemns us, where will we turn? We turn to Christ. We turn to the suffering and death of Christ—the blood of Christ. This is the only cleansing agent in the universe that can give the conscience relief in life and peace in death.
>
> —John Piper

The author of Hebrews used Old Testament images and rituals to convince believing Jews to remain faithful to Jesus. How would you explain Jesus' death to a nonreligious person? What images would you use? Why?

How do you feel about this emphasis on blood and sacrifices?

Why does God insist on establishing His covenants with blood?

How does the fact that the new covenant has replaced the old, outdated covenant play out in your life? Does it form the foundation for your relationship with God? If so, is it a foundation you take for granted or one that increases in value as you go through stormy periods of your life? Think about your response, and if you're in a group, explain your answer.

PRAYER ✠ Ask and Listen

Seek the face of God. Ask, "Lord, what are You saying to us today?"

Reread John Wesley's covenant prayer on page 57. Think about the changes it might call you to make. Listen for the Spirit's invitation to surrender your life to God.

CONTEMPLATION ✠ Reflect and Yield

Reflect on the changes God might call you to make in response to Wesley's covenant prayer. List any and all of your doubts, and surrender them to Jesus as you pray, "I am Yours, and You are mine."

GROUP STUDY

- What is the difference between the old and new covenant?

- Reread Hebrews 8:10-12. What are the benefits of the New Covenant?

- Are you experiencing these benefits in your own life? If so, how?

- What does it mean for our lives that Jesus is our High Priest?

- What impact does the shedding of Christ's blood have on all humanity?

- Write the covenant prayer of John Wesley on an index card. Carry this card with you during the week. At various times, pull the card out and breathe this prayer to God as a way of commitment to Him.

I HAVE COME TO DO YOUR WILL

LISTENING FOR GOD THROUGH
HEBREWS 10:1-18

SUMMARY

Jesus set the standard for submitting to God's will. One part of the mystery of the Incarnation is that Jesus had freedom of choice just like we do today. He was God, so He was in agreement with God's plan. At the same time, He was a human being with a free will that He needed to surrender to God's purpose.

Jesus learned to be obedient to His parents (Luke 2:51). Then in the Garden of Gethsemane, He surrendered His will to the Father's (Luke 22:42). Paul tells us in Philippians 2:8 that Jesus "became obedient to death—even death on a cross!" The author of Hebrews sums up Jesus' submissive attitude with the words "Here I am, I have come to do your will."

Jesus' sacrifice on the Cross makes us perfect while it makes us holy. As we follow in His footsteps, we learn to submit our will to God's will. As we do this, we discover the peace that comes when we surrender to God's will.

PREPARATION ✠ Focus Your Thoughts

Jesus prayed "Not my will but yours be done" three times. Why did God's Son need to pray this prayer? Why did He pray it more than once?

READING ✠ Hear the Word

The Trinity is seen working for our salvation in these verses. Hebrews 10:1-10 outlines God the Father's will for our salvation and sanctification through Jesus' sacrifice. Hebrews 10:11-14 shows us how God the Son made the final sacrifice that makes us holy. Hebrews 10:15-18 describes God the Spirit's work in changing our heart and reprogramming our minds.

There are two key phrases in this part of Hebrews.

Make perfect: In this context, to make someone perfect is to help him or her become and do what God intended.

Make holy: This phrase also can be translated *sanctify*. It is everything God does to make us more like Jesus. Sanctification makes us more like God designed us to be. At the same time, it makes us more like God.

MEDITATION ✟ Engage the Word

Meditate on Hebrews 10:1-4

The Law and rituals of the first covenant were unable to meet our needs. They could not make us what God wanted us to be. According to Hebrews 10:1, what was the reason for their shortfall? How does the endless repetition of the sacrifices prove they cannot make us what God intended us to be?

Observe a shadow for a minute or two. What can you learn about the reality behind it by watching the shadow? In what ways does the Law shadow the sacrifice of Jesus?

Why couldn't the blood of animals take away our sins? How would you have felt if you had been reminded of your sins year after year without ever receiving release from your guilt? What would you have wanted to do? Why?

Meditate on Hebrews 10:5-10

The author shows the contrast between sacrifices and Jesus' statement, "Here I am, I have come to do your will." How many reasons can you think of for God to desire Jesus' obedience more than animal sacrifices? What does this imply about your submission to God's will and your religious acts?

According to Hebrews 10:10, what was God's will? How are holiness and obedience connected? Are you holy because of what you do or because of what Jesus did? Think about the difference and the reasons for your answer. If you are participating in a group, discuss your conclusions.

Read the C. S. Lewis quote. Do you agree or disagree? Why? How would you summarize the central doctrine of Christianity? Would you be able to communicate it to a non-Christian? What would you say, and why?

> The central Christian belief is that Christ's death has somehow put us right with God and given us a fresh start.
>   —C. S. Lewis

Meditate on Hebrews 10:11-18

Use a chart to list the points of contrast between the animal sacrifices and Jesus' sacrifice. What would these differences mean to Jewish believers thinking about turning away from Jesus? What would be the result of turning away from Him?

Read the statement about Jesus' sacrifice. If Jesus is the final sacrifice for your sins, why do you need to submit your will to God? Reflect on your answer.

> [Jesus] became the final Priest and the final Sacrifice. Sinless, He did not offer sacrifices for himself. Immor-

tal, He never has to be replaced. Human, He could
bear human sins. Therefore, He did not offer sacrifices
for himself; He offered himself as the final sacrifice.

—John Piper

Hebrews 10:14 might be paraphrased this way: "By His one sacrifice on the Cross, Jesus has made us what God intended for us to be as long as we are becoming more and more like Him." How has Jesus enabled you to carry out what God planned for you? In what ways is He still in the process of changing you from the inside out?

Read the quote by John Piper. Are you encouraged by your "experienced progress"? Why, or why not? How is God inviting you to grow deeper in holiness?

Being sanctified means that we are imperfect and in
process. We are becoming holy—but we are not yet
fully holy. And it is precisely these—and only these—
who are already perfected. The joyous encouragement
here is that the evidence of our perfection before God
is not our experienced perfection, but our experienced
progress. *—John Piper*

Read the message taken from a church sign. How would you help an individual who knows the history of Jesus' death but not the salvation it provides? What recommendations would you make to help a person recognize his or her need and the way to move into a relationship with Jesus?

> Jesus died on the cross—that's history. Jesus died for
> me—that's salvation.   —A Church Sign

PRAYER † Ask and Listen

Seek the face of God. Ask, "Lord, what are You saying to us today?"

Pray Jesus' prayer found in this text: "Here I am, I have come to do your will." Listen for the Spirit's voice to give you an assignment.

CONTEMPLATION † Reflect and Yield

Jesus submitted to the Father's will to demonstrate God's love to us sinners. How is the Father asking you to share His love? How will you show kindness to others?

Group Study

- Describe a time in your life when you needed to pray the prayer: "Not my will but yours be done."

- When you surrendered your will to God, how did it help you become more at peace with your situation?

- How does our culture view "perfection"?

- Why is it crucial for us to get our understanding of "perfection" from the Bible, rather than from society?

- Do you feel you are in the process of "being made holy" by God? If so, how?

- How can you demonstrate and show God's love to someone this week? In each situation you face this week, silently say, "Here I am, I have come to do your will."

I WILL WORSHIP
LISTENING FOR GOD THROUGH
HEBREWS 12:14-29

SUMMARY

In our churches, and even our youth groups, we often disagree over the style of music or Biblical translation that will be used. These disputes usually skip over the real meaning of worshiping God. It is *whom* we worship and not *how* we worship that counts.

Worship is a lifestyle of love—a life of obedience to the two great commandments (Mark 12:28-31). It is a growing holiness that is so focused on Jesus and on what others need that it is glad to sacrifice. We worship best when we love God with all that we are and have while loving our neighbor as ourselves.

The hunger for peace and holiness is a necessity for every Christian. In these verses, you will take notice of a call to worship the Lord in the beauty of holiness.

PREPARATION ☦ FOCUS YOUR THOUGHTS

Complete these sentences one by one.

"I worship best at . . . (a place)."

"I worship best when . . . (a time)."

"I enjoy worship music that . . . (a style)."

"I used to think worship was . . . but now I realize it is . . . (a purpose)."

Reflect on your answers. If you are in a group, discuss your individual worship needs.

READING ☦ HEAR THE WORD

Read Hebrews 12:14-29. These terms will be important to know as you listen to this passage.

Make every effort: The King James Version translates this as *follow* while other translations say *strive for.* The idea involves running hard to reach a goal. Paul uses this illustration in Philippians 3:12 and 14 to compare the Christian life to a track race.

Peace: We often think of peace as living a life without troubles, but in the Bible it is far more. It is everything that contributes to human well-being. It grows out of living in obedience to God's principles (Prov. 3:1-2).

Holiness: This is an important attribute of God, but we can achieve it only in relative terms. God is absolutely holy, and we can become holy by being in His presence. Holiness will make us different from and separated from the world. We will learn to think, act, and relate to others as Jesus does.

Godless: This describes a person with no awareness of or interest in God. He or she is focused only on life in this world.

MEDITATION ☦ ENGAGE THE WORD

Meditate on Hebrews 12:14-17

The author commands readers to run hard to reach two goals. What are the goals we are striving to reach? Based on the definitions you just read, what actions might be involved in making an effort to reach those goals?

Read the quote by John Stott on page 72. Have you thought about the Christian life like he does? How would you describe the life of following Jesus? Brainstorm ways to illustrate this principle of commitment and spiritual maturity.

> *You become a Christian in a moment, but not a mature
> Christian. Christ can enter, cleanse, and forgive you in
> a matter of seconds, but it will take much longer for
> your character to be transformed and molded to His
> will. . . . When we receive Christ, a moment of commit-
> ment will lead to a lifetime of adjustment.*
>
> —John Stott

List the four things the writer of Hebrews says we should avoid. Compare these four things with the two goals we are to pursue. How are they different? How does this set of warnings relate to those you've seen before in Hebrews (2:1-4; 3:12—4:2; 5:11—6:8; 10:26-31)? Which one speaks to your heart most clearly? Why?

K. P. Yohannan refers to "cheap grace"—forgiveness without lifestyle changes. Do you agree that most Christians are not living lives that honor Jesus? What evidence can you share to support your answer?

> *The Bible says that the only way to see the face of the
> Living God is to be pure and to be purged from sin in
> our heart. This is the fact that is lost in the "cheap
> grace" gospel that has flooded our churches. And to-*

> *day, we are seeing the terrible fruit of this watered-*
> *down perversion of the truth—the world has swal-*
> *lowed the church. Most Christians are living carnal*
> *lives of defeat and failure.*   —K. P. Yohannan

Read the story of Jacob and Esau in Genesis 25. How does Esau's decision to trade his inheritance rights for food show us the things we need to avoid? Read Genesis 27. Why couldn't Esau inherit Isaac's blessing? What does this say in regards to those who turn away from Jesus?

In your opinion, which of the instructions given in Hebrews 12:14-17 is most relevant for Christians today? For what reasons? Which one do you need to pay attention to today?

Meditate on Hebrews 12:18-24

Draw a chart to contrast and compare the two mountains described in these verses. What is different about them? What is similar? What reasons for staying faithful to Jesus can be found in this contrast? If you are in a group, share your charts with one another.

Meditate on Hebrews 12:25-29

Who are we instructed to listen to? What will happen if we don't listen to Him? What will happen if we do? Which of these—the negative or the positive—is most motivating to you? Why?

What has God promised to do to the universe? What will happen to everything that cannot be shaken? What are we receiving? What does the author conclude about what we should do? How are we to respond to God's blessing? How can we worship God acceptably?

What examples of a "consuming fire" can you think of? Have you ever been near such a fire? What did it feel like? What was left behind after the fire passed?

Read the quote by David Bosch. Do you agree or disagree with Bosch's comment? How does this idea compare to the principles you've uncovered in Hebrews? Have you made "a decisive and irrevocable" turn toward God and others? Think about how the Holy Spirit brought you to the place where you made that decision. If you have not made that kind of turn toward God and your neighbor, what is holding you back? Can someone help you over the hump? If so, how?

> To become a disciple means a decisive and irrevocable turning to both God and neighbor. What follows from there is a journey which never ends in this life, a journey of continually discovering new dimensions of loving God and neighbor. —David J. Bosch

PRAYER ⸸ Ask and Listen

Seek the face of God. Ask, "Lord, what are You saying to us today?"

Silently invite the Holy Spirit to coach you on your pursuit of peace and holiness. Listen for His encouragement and correction as He shows you how to make a greater effort to reach your goals.

CONTEMPLATION ⸸ Reflect and Yield

Have you decided to keep on learning to love God and your neighbor? How has this commitment guided your thoughts about worship? Are you willing to surrender your preferences to help others connect with God?

GROUP STUDY

- Can you think of any instances in your own church when there were disagreements about the style of worship?

- How was this disagreement resolved? How did it affect your worship experience together in the future?

- Have each person describe their style of individual

worship. Reflect on how each person worships in different ways.

- Would you say that you are living a life that honors Jesus? If not, what could be done to change that?

- In your opinion, why is God a consuming fire? Is it because of His holiness, His love, or another attribute? Discuss this as a group.

- What has been the most influential concept you have learned through this study of Hebrews?

- How will it impact your life, as well as your relationship with God?

www.ingramcontent.com/pod-product-compliance
Lightning Source LLC
Chambersburg PA
CBHW071929020426
42331CB00010B/2780